BETSY ROSS

AND THE U.S. FLAG: SEPARATING FACT FROM FICTION

by Danielle Smith-Llera

CAPSTONE PRESS
a capstone imprint

Capstone Captivate is published by Capstone Press, an imprint of Capstone.
1710 Roe Crest Drive
North Mankato, Minnesota 56003
www.capstonepub.com

Library of Congress Cataloging-in-Publication Data is available on the Library of Congress website.
ISBN: 978-1-4966-9562-8 (library binding)
ISBN: 978-1-4966-9672-4 (paperback)
ISBN: 978-1-9771-5388-3 (eBook PDF)

Summary: Betsy Ross made many flags during the American Revolution. But did she sew the first flag? Follow the facts and explore the fiction in this tale of stars and stripes.

Image Credits
Alamy: Chronicle, 27; Bridgeman Images: © Look and Learn, 7; Dreamstime: Georgios Kollidas, 16; Getty Images: Bettmann, 25, Lambert, 24, Stock Montage, 17; Granger: 26, Sarin Images, 20; Library of Congress: cover (top right), 5, 11, 12, 13; Line of Battle Enterprise: 15; National Gallery of Art: Gift of Mr. and Mrs. George W. Davison, 23; Newscom: Everett Collection, cover (bottom left); North Wind Picture Archives: 8, 10, 18 (left), 21; Shutterstock: David Smart, cover (top left), back cover, 14, Everett Collection, cover (bottom right), 18 (right), f11photo, 6, Joseph Sohm, 22, Lee Snider Photo Images, 28, Yuriy Boyko, 9; Smithsonian Institution: National Portrait Gallery, 19

Editorial Credits
Editor: Gena Chester; Designer: Kyle Grenz; Media Researcher: Svetlana Zhurkin; Production Specialist: Katy LaVigne

Source Notes
p. 4, "I don't know, but I will try," "First American Flag History," Historic Philadelphia, n.d., historicphiladelphia.org/betsy-ross-house/flag/
p. 16, "Hopkinson was not the only person consulted," Marla R. Miller. *Betsy Ross and the Making of America*. New York: Henry Holt, 2010, p. 180.
p. 17, "new constellation," "Today in History - June 14: Flag Day," Library of Congress, n.d., loc.gov/item/today-in-history/june-14/
p. 17, "scattered," "Affidavit of Rachel Fletcher, a daughter of Elizabeth Claypoole (Betsy Ross)," Betsy Ross and the American Flag, July 31, 1871, ushistory.org/betsy/flagaffs.html
p. 28, "First Flag of the US Made in this House," "History of the Betsy Ross House," Historic Philadelphia, n.d., historicphiladelphia.org/betsy-ross-house/house/
p. 28, "like the Revolution it represents, was the work of many hands," *Betsy Ross and the Making of America*, p. 181.

All internet sites appearing in back matter were available and accurate when this book was sent to press.

Printed and bound in the USA. PO#3837

Table of Contents

Words in **bold** are in the glossary.

Introduction

It was May 1776. The American Revolution against Great Britain was entering its second year. Away from the battlefront, three men paid a visit to 24-year-old Betsy Ross's workshop in Philadelphia. The men were **delegates** to the Continental Congress, the government of the 13 American colonies. They wanted a new flag to unify Americans.

Ross was a skilled **upholsterer**. She sewed items such as curtains and furniture coverings. One of the men showed her a sketch. He was George Washington, commander of the Continental Army. Washington asked Ross if she could sew a flag with 13 stripes and 13 six-point stars. Ross replied, "I don't know, but I will try." She snipped paper to show that five-point stars were simpler to cut. By June, Ross had finished the first U.S. flag. Its five-point stars were arranged in a circle.

An illustration from the early 1900s of Betsy Ross presenting the finished flag to George Washington

Ross's meeting with the delegates is now famous in U.S. history. But did it actually take place? Did Ross really make the first U.S. flag? Follow along to find out what is fact and what is fiction.

Chapter One

Looking for Clues

Historians have no proof that the **legendary** visit took place at all. Neither Washington, nor the other two men, ever recorded it in letters or journals. No journal or letters written by Ross exist. Historians are also missing documents to prove exactly where the meeting would have taken place.

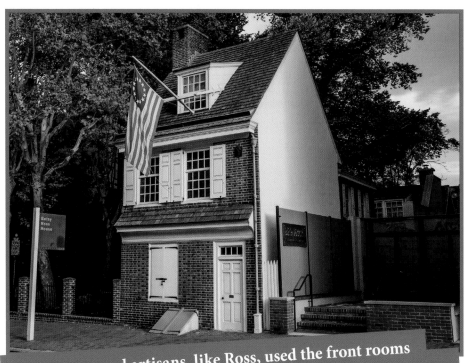

Shopkeepers and artisans, like Ross, used the front rooms of their homes as a workshop and showroom for customers.

Historians have found no document that proves Ross sewed the first U.S. flag. There is no shop **receipt** that makes it a fact. The first document historians have found that mentions the new flag design is an official record of the Continental Congress. It is dated June 14, 1777—a year after the rumored visit. It proves that Congress approved the design, but it does not include Ross's name.

Congress approved the new U.S. flag on June 14, 1777. June 14 is now celebrated as Flag Day.

Sending Signals

Ross did own an upholstery business. But historians have not found any newspaper articles about Ross doing a special flag project during this time. In 1776, making a flag would not have made headlines. Flags were not the symbols of **patriotism** we view them as today.

American patriots fought British soldiers under the pine tree flag at the Battle of Bunker Hill in 1775.

Instead, flags were practical. They were used to communicate. They flew on ships and forts. They were also carried by soldiers into battle. The colors and shapes on flags helped tell whether enemies or **allies** were near.

The Grand Union flag

FLAG FAILURE

George Washington tried to introduce a new flag in January 1776. He had the Grand Union flag raised by his Continental Army near Boston. It included 13 red and white stripes to represent the united colonies. But it also included a section that looked like Great Britain's flag. This design flaw made it look like the Americans were surrendering to British forces.

Chapter Two

Big News

Even though there isn't much proof it really happened, Ross herself told the story of the 1776 shop visit to family members. If the meeting did take place, it would have been an amazing story. She got to meet Washington, victorious leader of the American Revolution and first president of the United States. Ross's relatives remembered her telling the story.

According to Ross family affidavits, Ross convinced Washington to use a five-point star instead of a six-point star.

Around 100 years after the visit, several relatives wrote it down as **affidavits** and swore they had heard it from Ross herself. The **accounts** are not historical facts. Today's version of the story is based on them.

A painting of Betsy Ross sewing the flag

In 1870, Ross's story went public. Her grandson William Canby gave a speech about it to the Historical Society of Pennsylvania. Historian Marla Miller believes Ross's relatives spoke out because they were worried that history would forget her. In the early to mid-1800s, history books about women who contributed to the American Revolution did not include Ross. The first book about the U.S. flag did not include her either.

People accepted Canby's story—even without facts to support it. Many were excited to hear Canby's story about the creation of the flag. But that's because people in the 1800s viewed the flag much differently than people did in 1776.

During the War of 1812, a huge U.S. flag over Fort McHenry in Baltimore, Maryland, inspired poet Francis Scott Key. He wrote the poem "Defence of Fort M'Henry." This was later turned into "The Star-Spangled Banner," the U.S. national anthem. In the 1860s, people began to fly their own U.S. flags with pride. During the Civil War, many people in the North felt the flag represented unity and pride. The flag was now a patriotic symbol.

Francis Scott Key wrote the poem "Defence of Fort M'Henry" after watching the battle from a boat in 1814.

At the time of Canby's speech, the United States was also getting ready for its 100-year anniversary of independence. A popular magazine published Canby's story in 1873. Ross's name soon became well known. Soon after, her story was included in history lessons in schools.

PICTURING BETSY ROSS

In the 1890s, Philadelphia painter Charles H. Weisgerber painted an enormous canvas titled *Birth of Our Nation's Flag*. He based it on the Ross family affidavits. For 40 years, the painting traveled to exhibitions around the country. Weisgerber also sold millions of small copies to raise money to keep the Betsy Ross House from being torn down.

Chapter Three

A Doubtful Tale?

Historians wonder if Ross and her descendants exaggerated her role in the new flag's design. There are no facts that prove Ross influenced the flag's design.

Historians do have proof that the flag's red and white stripes were not Ross's idea. The design came from a flag used by the Continental Army. But the affidavit by Ross's daughter, Rachel Fletcher, reports that her mother changed the stripes' length. It says Ross switched the square-shaped design to a rectangular one.

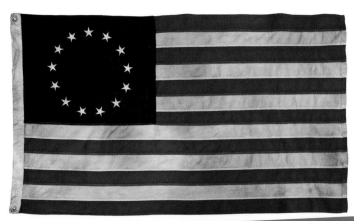

The 13 stars and stripes on the flag popularly attributed to Betsy Ross represented the original 13 colonies.

George Washington became commander of the Continental Army on June 14, 1775.

The flag's white stars on a blue background were not Ross's idea either. This color scheme was taken from a blue flag Washington used as commander of the army.

Fact!

A five-point paper star believed to belong to Ross was discovered in the 1920s. It was inside a safe once owned by Samuel Wetherill, one of Ross's friends.

Taking Credit

There is only one document about flag-making in Congress's records. In 1780, politician Francis Hopkinson asked for payment from Congress for designing the first flag for Navy ships. However, Congress refused to pay him because "Hopkinson was not the only person consulted" on the design. Unfortunately, no other names were mentioned.

Today, there is no known record of Hopkinson's or Ross's designs. When Congress approved the first U.S. flag in 1777, they weren't specific about the design.

Francis Hopkinson

The documentation stated only that 13 stars should appear on a blue background in a "new constellation." If Ross arranged stars in a circle, there is no existing flag from her shop—or description by someone who saw one—to prove it. But her daughter's affidavit does provide a clue why she would. Ross had told her daughter that the stars looked "scattered" in Washington's sketch.

Fact!

Flag makers could arrange stars on U.S. flags however they wished—until 1912. That's when President William Taft required they be arranged into rows.

Two Problems

According to Ross family affidavits, the three visitors to Ross's shop were on official business for Congress. They were George Ross, Robert Morris, and George Washington. The three visitors left Ross's shop with a small example of the new design to present to Congress. However, Congress's records at the time do not include discussion about a new flag. And facts suggest it is unlikely two of those three men were ever there.

George Ross

Robert Morris

Congress in 1776

George Ross was not a member of Congress until August 1776—three months after Betsy Ross claimed they visited her. It is unlikely Congress would have sent a nonmember to do official business.

Unlike George Ross, Morris was a member of Congress in May. But at the time, he did not support independence from Great Britain. In July 1776, he did not vote for it. It is unlikely he would have helped find a flag for a new nation two months before this.

Chapter Four

A Probable Tale

Historians have also found evidence that shows Betsy Ross's story could be true. Advertisements in newspapers at the time prove that Philadelphia had many upholstery shops. Upholsterers served customers who could afford to decorate homes with fine fabrics. But they also served the needs of the military. They sewed tents, uniforms, and pouches to hold gunpowder. Making flags was part of the job.

Many illustrations of Betsy Ross show her sitting peacefully and sewing, but her work was much more physically demanding.

George Ross would have had personal reasons for choosing Betsy Ross's shop for the project. George's nephew was Betsy's husband and business partner, John Ross. John Ross had died in January 1776. George Ross might have wanted

A man and a woman shopping at a store in the late 1700s

to help Betsy by bringing new business to her shop. He could also trust her loyalty to the Revolution. This was important because making the new flag was **treason** under British law.

Fact!

Female business owners did not have the same rights and power as male business owners during Ross's lifetime. Because of this, Ross's business was known under her husband's name, John Ross.

Exciting Clues

Historians cannot prove that George Washington actually visited Ross's shop in May 1776. But they have found evidence that it's possible.

Washington and Ross knew each other before 1776. Church records show they attended the same church and sat near each other. Ross family affidavits say Ross sewed ruffles for Washington's shirts. But in 2015, real proof was finally discovered. Staff at Washington's Virginia home found a 1774 receipt for sheets, bed canopies, and other bedding items from "John Ross of Philadelphia"—Betsy's husband.

George Washington's home at Mount Vernon, Virginia

George Washington

Washington was in Philadelphia in May 1776. Congress's records and Washington's own letters prove it. He purchased supplies, including tents, from another Philadelphia upholstery shop.

Busy Flag Maker

A receipt for a flag created in Ross's shop in mid-1776 would be an exciting find. It would help prove the Betsy Ross story is not a legend. Yet other receipts have already convinced some that Betsy Ross's story could be true.

Receipts from the early 1800s prove that Ross became a leading Philadelphia flag maker. She and a team of family members made more than 50 enormous flags. They were purchased by the government to fly over forts along the Schuylkill River during the War of 1812.

Betsy Ross and her assistants sewing a U.S. flag

A ship with American flags docked in Philadelphia in 1800

Just one document proves Ross was making flags during the Revolution. Notes from a meeting of the Pennsylvania Navy Board on May 29, 1777, mention Ross. This proves she was paid to sew flags for Pennsylvania state ships. But there's no proof of payment for the first U.S. flag for Congress.

Fact!

It is possible that clues about Ross's work during the Revolution were destroyed. A fire burned the records kept in Philadelphia's War Department in 1800.

Chapter Five

The Real Betsy

The popular story that began with the Ross family affidavits does not match important facts about her life. Writers and painters in the late 1800s showed Ross as a seamstress quietly sewing a flag at home. But this was not her life in the 1700s—or the life of other upholsterers.

Ross's job involved tough physical work. She stuffed mattresses. She crafted enormous flags that were 18 by 24 feet (5.5 by 7.3 meters) in size.

UPHOLSTERER, In Chestnut-street, near Second-street, PHILADELPHIA, MAKES all Sorts of Uphol-sterers Work, in the neatest and newest Fashions, at the most reasonable Prices, such as Beds and Window Curtains, Easy Chairs, Couches; Matrasses, either of Hair or Wool, Feather Beds, Sacking Bottoms, Chair Bottoms and Ship Stools, &c. &c.

Those that are pleased to fa-vour him with their Custom, may depend on Care and Dis-patch. Tbc. 6 W.

PENNSYLVANIA GAZETTE

A newspaper advertisement that lists types of work offered by an upholsterer from Philadelphia in 1765

Ross was also a clever businesswoman who made a steady supply of flags for the government. She outlived three husbands and provided for her large extended family. She worked in her busy shop into her mid-70s. She only retired when her eyesight grew too weak.

Betsy Ross

An Unforgettable Story

Betsy Ross's story traveled from her lips to her children and grandchildren—and to generations of people. In 1876, the people who lived in the house where it was thought Ross had worked put up a sign. Its message sounded like a fact: "First Flag of the US Made in this House." Today, around 250,000 people visit the building each year. It's now called the Betsy Ross House. The museum refers to Ross affectionately as the "First Lady of the Stars & Stripes."

Historians suspect the story of the first U.S. flag involves others besides Ross. Historian Marla Miller explains that the flag, "like the Revolution it represents, was the work of many hands." But for historians like Miller, that fact does not change the importance of patriotic, hardworking, and creative Betsy Ross in early U.S. history.

Sign in front of the Betsy Ross House on Arch Street

The Betsy Ross Flag Story

Fiction Betsy Ross made the first U.S. flag.

Fact As an upholsterer, Ross made flags and other items used by the military.

Fiction George Washington was part of the group that visited Betsy Ross's Philadelphia upholstery shop in May 1776.

Fact Receipts show that Washington was in Philadelphia buying supplies and equipment for the Continental Army.

Fiction Robert Morris was part of the group that visited Betsy Ross's Philadelphia upholstery shop.

Fact Morris's role in this visit seems doubtful since he did not support independence from Great Britain at that time.

Fiction George Ross was part of the group that visited Betsy Ross's Philadelphia upholstery shop.

Fact George Ross was not a member of Congress in May 1776.

Fiction Betsy Ross is responsible for the five-point stars in today's U.S. flag.

Fact When Congress approved a new flag design in 1777, it did not specify the number of points the stars should have.

Glossary

account (uh-KOWNT)—an official statement explaining actions or experiences

affidavit (a-fih-DAY-vit)—a written statement signed by the author who swears the information is true

ally (AL-lie)—a person or party who has agreed to protect another

delegate (DEL-uh-guht)—a person sent by a group as a representative

legendary (LEH-juhn-dayr-ee)—famous due to a unique characteristic

patriotism (PAY-tree-uh-tism)—loyalty toward a nation or leaders of that nation

receipt (re-SEET)—a written document that proves money or goods were received

treason (TREE-zen)—the crime of trying to overthrow one's own government

upholsterer (up-OLS-stur-ur)—someone trained to create and repair the fabric in furniture and household pieces

Read More

Chang, Kirsten. *The United States Flag*. Minneapolis: Bellwether Media, Inc., 2019.

Grove, Tim. *Star-Spangled: The Story of a Flag, a Battle, and the American Anthem*. New York: Abrams Books for Young Readers, 2020.

Morlock, Rachael. *The Real Story behind the Founding Fathers*. New York: PowerKids Press, 2020.

Internet Sites

Flag of the United States Facts for Kids
kids.kiddle.co/Flag_of_the_United_States

The History of the American Flag
pbs.org/a-capitol-fourth/history/old-glory/

Index